An Imprint of Pop!
popbooksonline.com

The Eras of Taylor Swift

THE 1989 era

Track List

1. Welcome to New York
2. Blank Space
3. Style
4. Out of the Woods
5. All You Had to Do Was Stay
6. Shake It Off
7. I Wish You Would
8. Bad Blood
9. Wildest Dreams
10. How You Get the Girl
11. This Love
12. I Know Places
13. Clean

by Grace Hansen

WELCOME TO DiscoverRoo!

This book is filled with videos, puzzles, games, and more! Scan the QR codes* while you read, or visit the website below to make this book pop.

popbooksonline.com/1989-era

abdobooks.com

Published by Pop!, a division of ABDO, PO Box 398166, Minneapolis, Minnesota 55439.

Printed in the United States of America, North Mankato, Minnesota.

082025
012026

Cover Photo: Alexandra Tarasova (BigArtLab); Shutterstock Images
Interior Photos: Alamy; AP Images; Everett Collection; Getty Images; Shutterstock; PaoloV/Flickr
Editors: Elizabeth Andrews and Anna Schwartz
Series Designer: Laura Graphenteen

Library of Congress Control Number: 2025941049

Publisher's Cataloging-in-Publication Data

Names: Hansen, Grace, author.
Title: The 1989 era / by Grace Hansen
Description: Minneapolis, Minnesota : Pop!, 2026 | Series: The eras of Taylor Swift | Includes online resources and index
Identifiers: ISBN 9781098248673 (lib. bdg.) | ISBN 9781098249199 (ebook)
Subjects: LCSH: Swift, Taylor, 1989- --Juvenile literature. | Popular music--Juvenile literature. | Popular (Songs, etc.)--Juvenile literature. | Albums--Juvenile literature. | Concerts--Juvenile literature. | Mass media and music--Juvenile literature.
Classification: DDC 782.42164092--dc23

*Scanning QR codes requires a web-enabled smart device with a QR code reader app and a camera.

TABLE OF CONTENTS

CHAPTER 1

TAYLOR TAKES ON POP

While Taylor Swift was on tour for her fourth album, *Red*, she began writing songs for what would be *1989*. She didn't know it yet, but her fifth album would take her from country music star to pop music icon.

WATCH A VIDEO HERE!

Meet Taylor

Birthday: December 13, 1989
Star Sign: Sagittarius
Place of Birth: West Reading, PA
Favorite Number: 13
Favorite Color: Purple
Favorite Meal: Chicken tenders and a chocolate shake

13

XOXO

Olivia Benson

***Taylor explained on* The Talk *that her best friend Ed Sheeran was the first person to hear* 1989.**

On August 18, 2014, the album's lead **single**, "Shake It Off," hit radio waves. People loved the catchy, dance-pop song. It was a new sound for Taylor, but fans loved it!

Over the following months, six more singles followed. Each had an accompanying music video. "Blank Space," the second single, sat firmly at number one on the Billboard Hot 100 for seven straight weeks. And the music video, featuring a sprawling mansion, white horses, and glamorous dresses, was the album's most popular.

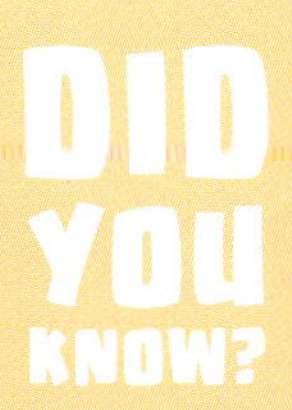

Taylor has the most Album of the Year wins at the **Grammy Awards**. She won for *Fearless*, *1989*, *folklore*, and *Midnights*.

CHAPTER 2

BORN IN *1989*

Taylor Swift's much-anticipated fifth album was released on October 27, 2014. *1989* was titled after Taylor's birth year. It was also a **symbolic** rebirth for Taylor, who **debuted** an entirely new sound. Her previous album, *Red*, was described by

EXPLORE LINKS HERE!

Polaroid camera sales spiked after fans saw the* 1989 *cover art.

some **critics** as "epic." Rather than trying to match that success with the same sound, Taylor changed it up completely.

Taylor said that *1989* came together naturally. She had not planned on creating a **synth-pop** album. But she loved that it had its own sound and was **cohesive** from beginning to end. When asked if she was worried about what fans would think of the new sound, she said, "The only thing people necessarily need is quality."

Taylor and her producers Max Martin (left) and Shellback (right) in the studio.

Taylor and her **producers** combined synthesizers, drum machines, and catchy melodies and refrains to create *1989*. Taylor sings most of the vocals on the album in her **alto** range.

Taylor performed a 1989 concert in Times Square on October 30, 2014.

The album kicks off with the incredible energy of "Welcome to New York." Taylor said the song has "bright, wide-eyed **optimism**." It sets the tone for the rest of *1989*.

Taylor worked with Imogen Heap on "Clean." Taylor wrote the lyrics and

Polaroids, neon signs, and boom boxes were popular in the 1980s.

melody for the song, and it took just two takes to record. She wrote "This Love" entirely on her own.

Hidden Message

The hidden message in the lyrics of "This Love" is "Timing is a funny thing." Taylor has explained that the song was written after she had a dream about an ex. Fans think the song could be about Jake Gyllenhaal or Harry Styles.

Antonoff accepted the Best Pop Vocal Album at the 58th Annual Grammys on behalf of Swift. He called her to share the news!

Producer Jack Antonoff created the instrumental for "Out of the Woods." He sent it to Taylor, and about 60 minutes later she replied with a voice note singing the complete lyrics. It was the first time that Taylor's songwriting came after the existing track.

Taylor's* 1989 *style was chic, modern, and playful.

DID YOU KNOW?

The Target Deluxe Edition of *1989* features Taylor's voice notes for song ideas. She wanted to share her process.

CHAPTER 3

BEHIND THE LYRICS

Many people see *1989* as an empowering album. Songs on previous albums often had lyrics describing Taylor's struggles and hurt. In *1989*, she is learning who she really is and celebrating her independence and happiness. The best example of this is comparing "Mean" from *Speak Now* to *1989*'s "Shake It Off."

COMPLETE AN ACTIVITY HERE!

Taylor said she is most creative and inspired to write when she is under pressure.

In "Mean," Taylor asks how someone can be so cruel to her for no reason. In "Shake It Off," Taylor proves that she can move past the haters in a fun and easy way.

Hidden Message

The hidden message in "Shake It Off" is "She danced to forget him."

Taylor said that she began writing "Blank Space" as a joke. She wanted to write a song based on if everything the media wrote about her was true. Taylor was often described as desperate and crazy. People said she moved on too quickly after each failed relationship. Taylor thought the character people created was actually quite interesting. She said it was helpful to laugh about the things that once bothered her.

The car featured in the "Blank Space" music video was a rare vintage Shelby AC Cobra.

Taylor opened the 2014 American Music Awards with a theatrical performance of "Blank Space."

Taylor and Harry Styles dated for a few months between late 2012 and early 2013.

Taylor described the anxiety-inducing yet catchy "Out of the Woods" as the song that "best represents [*1989*]." The sound and feel of the song perfectly mirror how Taylor felt in a relationship that the song is based on. "The whole time we were having happy memories or crazy memories or ridiculously anxious times, in my head it was just like, 'Are we OK yet? Are we there yet? Are we out of this yet?'" Taylor recalled.

BASED ON TRUE EVENTS

Fans were surprised by the "Out of the Woods" lyrics, "Remember when you hit the brakes too soon? / Twenty stitches in the hospital room." Taylor said that the lyrics were based on true events. She wrote them to prove that people do not know everything about her.

Taylor's street style has often reflected the era that she is in.

CHAPTER 4

REINVENTED & RECLAIMED

Before *1989* even dropped, Taylor hosted fans for live listening parties. The *1989* Secret Sessions were held at Taylor's homes in Los Angeles, New York, Nashville, and Rhode Island. She also had people to her hotel room in London. Taylor said that having people to her home felt cozy

LEARN MORE HERE!

and comfortable. The lucky fans were handpicked by Taylor. She shared the complete album with them as well as explanations about each song.

Taylor's short hair became a defining look of her* 1989 *Era.

Taylor wore sunglasses and a sequined bomber jacket for the tour's opening number, "Welcome to New York."

The 1989 World Tour kicked off on May 5, 2015, in Tokyo, Japan. Tickets for some cities sold out within minutes, causing Taylor to add more shows. In

the end, Taylor performed an amazing 85 concerts. Fans and **critics** alike praised the show from beginning to end.

DID YOU KNOW?

The 1989 World Tour was the highest-grossing concert of 2015.

Taylor's beaded Roberto Cavalli two-piece set came in several colors.

1989 was the eighth act in Taylor's Eras Tour concert. The set opened with a neon city skyline. Taylor and her dancers rose from below the stage.

Taylor appeared in a shiny, two-piece set and matching boots. The outfit was like the one she wore during the album's tour. It helped Taylor fully embrace her pop era! Not surprisingly, the album got a lot of stage time. Taylor chose to feature the songs "Style," "Blank Space," "Shake It Off," "Wildest Dreams," and "Bad Blood."

Taylor revealed a fresh 1989 Era look for the European leg of her tour.

At her final Los Angeles show at SoFi Stadium, Taylor announced her re-recorded album, *1989 (Taylor's Version)*. She also shared that the album would include five From the Vault tracks. These were songs that she wrote during the *1989* Era but didn't put on the final album. Her refreshed 1980s-inspired, **synth-pop** album **debuted** on October 27, 2023.

Taylor stated, "I was born in 1989, reinvented for the first time in 2014, and a part of me was reclaimed in 2023...."

In its debut week,* 1989 (Taylor's Version) *sold more than 1.6 million copies.

MAKING CONNECTIONS

TEXT-TO-SELF

What is your favorite song from the *1989* Era? Why is it your favorite?

TEXT-TO-TEXT

Have you read books about any other music artists? How are they similar to or different from Taylor Swift?

TEXT-TO-WORLD

As a reader, why do you think so many people around the world connect with Taylor Swift and her music? Write a few sentences to explain your answer.

GLOSSARY

alto — the lowest vocal range for the female voice and the highest for a male voice.

cohesive — in the arts, describing something that feels whole from beginning to end.

critic — a person whose job is to judge music, movies, plays, art, or literature.

debut — to appear for the first time.

Grammy Awards — an event that recognizes and awards remarkable works in music throughout the year.

optimism — a habit of expecting everything to turn out for the best.

producer — a person who organizes the creation of music recordings.

single — a song that is released as a stand-alone from the album.

symbolic — acting as a symbol. A symbol is an object or image that represents something else.

synth-pop — a type of music that uses synthesizers and other electronic instruments, originating in the early 1980s.

INDEX